30 FUN WAYS to Learn About WRITING

ANN ROBERTS
ILLUSTRATED BY K. WHELAN DERY

© 2011 Gryphon House, Inc.
Published by Gryphon House, Inc.
10770 Columbia Pike, Suite 201
Silver Spring, MD 20901
800.638.0928; 301.595.9500; 301.595.0051 (fax)

Visit us on the web at www.gryphonhouse.com

Originally published in 2009 by A&C Black Publishers Limited.

All rights reserved. No part of this publication may be reproduced, stored in a retrieval system, or transmitted in any form or by any means, electronic, mechanical, photocopying, recording or otherwise, without the prior written permission of the publisher. Printed in China through Asia Pacific Offset. Every effort has been made to locate copyright and permission information.

Illustrations: K. Whelan Dery
Cover Art: © iStockphoto LP 2009. All rights reserved. iStockphoto® and iStock® are trademarks of iStockphoto LP. Flash® is a registered trademark of Adobe Inc. www.istockphoto.com.

Library of Congress Cataloging-in-Publication Data
30 fun ways to learn about writing / by Ann Roberts . . . [et al.].
     p. cm.
  Includes index.
  ISBN 978-0-87659-366-0
  1. Language arts (Elementary)—Activity programs. 2. Composition (Language arts) 3. English language—Composition and exercises—Study and teaching (Elementary). I. Roberts, Ann. II. Title: Thirty fun ways to learn about writing.
  LB1576.T497 2011
  372.62'3--dc22
                              2010045550

Bulk purchase
Gryphon House books are available for special premiums and sales promotions as well as for fund-raising use. Special editions or book excerpts also can be created to specification. For details, contact the Director of Marketing at Gryphon House.

Disclaimer
Gryphon House, Inc. and the author cannot be held responsible for damage, mishap, or injury incurred during the use of or because of activities in this book. Appropriate and reasonable caution and adult supervision of children involved in activities and corresponding to the age and capability of each child involved is recommended at all times. Do not leave children unattended at any time. Observe safety and caution at all times.

30 Fun Ways to Learn About Writing

by Ann Roberts

With contributions from Linda Andrews, Sonora, California; Virginia Jean Herrod, Columbia, South Carolina; and Gail Morris, Kemah, Texas.

Contents

Introduction 7
    Learning Objectives 8

Activities
    All About Me 12
    Your Name's the Game 14
    I Like It! 16
    Bag It! 18
    Make a List 20
    Remember This! 22
    Make a License Plate 24
    Send a Message 26
    The Magic Cookbook 28
    A Toy Story 30
    Let's Write About It 32
    Lost and Found 34
    Squishy Bags 36
    Wish You Were Here! 38
    Morning Journals 40
    Secrets and Spies 42
    So Many Languages 44
    Long, Long Ago 46
    Signs of Writing 48
    Let's Go on a Visit! 50
    Going My Way? 52
    In Character 54
    Seeds "R" Us 56
    Going to the Hospital 58
    Fire, Fire! 60
    May I Take a Message? 62
    Staying at a Hotel 64
    Ticket, Please! 66

When Can You Come? 68
RSVP 70

Index 73

Introduction

Most children acquire speech naturally by interacting with adults and the other children in their environment. But in order to become writers, children must develop the concept of message. They then compose, write, and present messages, using a range of physical and mental skills. The decoding and writing of symbols is a highly complicated activity. Children need to have plenty of exposure to symbols in their environment and in written language before they can begin to imitate or replicate them. Of the four language modes (talking, listening, reading, and writing), fluency in writing is the most complex and the last to develop.

Young children learn best through play and imitation. They learn about the nature and purpose of writing by:

- Observing adults and other children writing (models of writers).
- Observing and noticing print in the environment (examples of writing).
- Sending and receiving messages in cards, letters, postcards, and notes (recognizing the value of writing for sending a message).
- Observing writing in books and other printed material (seeing the difference between pictures and print).
- Experimenting with mark-making and writing (trying to write, and seeing themselves as writers).

From a very young age, children begin to recognize the elements of writing, particularly those associated with their own names. They make marks that approximate the symbols they see—straight lines, radials, circles, and dots—to represent letters. Wiggly lines, zigzags, and rows of marks all represent the lines and blocks in our writing. This stage is often referred to as "emergent" writing. It develops best through free experimentation.

Two key components to ensure children's success are: first, supportive adults; and, second, interesting opportunities that stimulate the children's excitement, curiosity, and imagination.

The ideas in this book cultivate interest in and curiosity about writing by setting up a variety of situations that are introduced and modeled by teachers, then offered to the children so they can develop the ideas in their free play.

Of course, in order to become confident and fluent writers, children also need to develop:
- Self-confidence, so they have the courage to take risks and make mistakes,
- Fine-motor control and coordination,
- Hand-eye coordination,
- Skill in handling a range of tools,

- Recognition of patterns and shapes, and
- The vocabulary of writing.

It is easy for adults to be distracted from encouraging independence in writing. It is easy to confuse handwriting and creative writing. Handwriting is a skill, needing close supervision and clear instruction—it must be taught. The writing described in this book is independent and is learned by confident children who have been encouraged to experiment, explore, imitate, and play with writing.

Here are some questions you might ask yourself about how your classroom supports children's writing:
- Is the classroom full of lists, labels, notices, and charts (examples of writing in different forms)?
- Are some of these written by children?
- Does the dramatic play area have relevant writing materials (pens, pads, forms, notebooks, and appointment books)?
- Does the classroom have magazines, junk mail, cookbooks, lists, and posters to demonstrate a range of writing? Are these materials available in a range of languages?
- Are there writing and reading spaces in the classroom? Do children and adults use them?
- Do I model writing for children? Do I write when and where children can see me?
- Do I provide writing and mark-making implements (pens, pencils, clipboards, whiteboards, paper, envelopes, and computers)?
- Are indoor and outdoor writing experiences supported?
- And most of all—do I make writing fun?

Learning Objectives

The activities, dramatic play situations, and games in this book support the following learning objectives.

Personal, Social, and Emotional Development

Children will:
- Be confident to try new activities, initiate ideas, and speak in a familiar group.
- Work as part of a group or class, taking turns and sharing fairly.
- Select and use activities and resources independently.
- Be attentive listeners, responding to what they have heard with appropriate actions.

Language, Communication, and Literacy

Children will:
- Interact with others, negotiating plans and activities and taking turns in conversation.
- Enjoy listening to and using spoken and written language, and readily turn to them in their play and learning.

30 Fun Ways to Learn About Writing

- Listen with enjoyment and respond to stories, songs and other music, rhymes and poems, and make up their own stories, rhymes, and poems.
- Retell narratives in the correct sequence.
- Extend their vocabularies, exploring the meanings and sounds of new words.
- Speak clearly and audibly with confidence and control.
- Use language to imagine and recreate roles and experiences.
- Use talk to organize, sequence, and clarify thinking, ideas, feelings, and events.
- Use their phonetic knowledge to write simple, familiar words and make phonetically plausible attempts at more complex words.
- Explore and experiment with sounds, words, and texts.
- Link letters and sounds, naming and sounding all the letters of the alphabet.
- Know that print and other written language carries meaning and, in English, is read from left to right and top to bottom.
- Show an understanding of the elements of a story, such as the main character and the sequence of events.
- Begin to understand how to find information in nonfiction texts.
- Attempt writing for various purposes, using features of different forms such as lists, stories, and instructions.
- Write their names and begin to write simple sentences.
- Hold and use a pencil effectively to form recognizable letters.

Knowledge and Understanding of the World

Children will:

- Find out about past and present events in their own lives and in those of their families and other people they know.
- Observe, find out about, and identify features of the place they live and in the natural world.

Creative Development

Children will:

- Express and communicate their ideas through designs.

Writing Activities

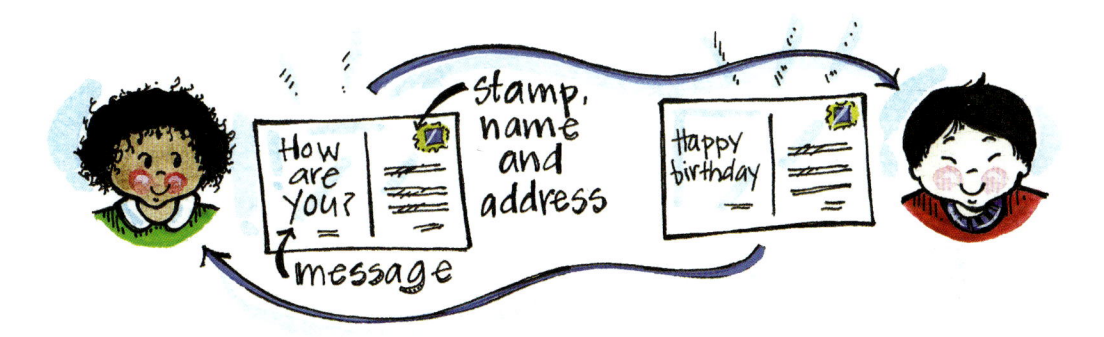

1 All About Me

Provide props the children can use for writing about themselves, describing details of their lives, writing diaries, making appointments, and sending cards.

Vocabulary

birthday
black
blue
brown
date
days of the week
eyes
green
hair
height
long
months of the year
shorter
skin
taller

What you need

- bathroom scales, yard sticks, and tape measures
- blank homemade books, 1 per child
- celebration cards
- charts for measuring height
- diaries, calendars, and birthday books
- display board or wall
- large mirror
- lists of family members and their pictures
- pens and pencils
- pictures of children from different countries
- posters or diagrams of children's bodies with parts labeled
- word lists of days, months, and times

Learning objectives

Children will:

- Speak clearly and audibly with confidence and control.
- Attempt writing for various purposes.
- Hold and use a pencil effectively to form recognizable letters.
- Look closely at similarities, differences, patterns, and change.

Before you start

Ask the children's families to send in pictures and names of the children's family members.

30 Fun Ways to Learn About Writing

What you do

1. Talk about and compare things such as the children's facial features, hair and skin color, birthday months, shoe sizes, family members, and height.
2. Compare this information and make charts.
3. Use mirrors to help the children look at and record their own features.
4. Collect information, such as phone numbers, addresses, and birthdays, for each child.
5. Write birthday cards for children and family members.
6. Encourage the children to make their own books about themselves with information of their choosing.

More ideas

- Link this activity to outside challenges in running, jumping, and throwing. Collect the results on a clipboard or flip chart.
- Take pictures of the children and use the pictures to inspire their writing.

30 Fun Ways to Learn About Writing

2 Your Name's the Game

Learning the mechanics of writing is a process. Help children gain confidence by writing their own names.

Vocabulary

alphabet
label
letter
lowercase
name
uppercase
word
write

What you need

- *Chicka Chicka Boom Boom* by Bill Martin, Jr. and John Archambault or another book about the alphabet
- computer labels (1 sheet per child)
- markers

Learning objectives

Children will:
- Write their names.
- Hold and use a pencil effectively to form recognizable letters.

Before you start

Read *Chicka Chicka Boom Boom* by Bill Martin, Jr. and John Archambault, or another book about the alphabet. Review the letters of the alphabet with the children.

What you do

❶ Explain to the children that they will write their names on labels and that you will put these on their artwork and belongings.

❷ Help the children make name labels using markers and sheets of computer labels.

❸ At this age, children are experimenting with written language. Some children will be able to write letters while others will express themselves with something that resembles scribbles rather than distinguishable letters. Regardless of their stage of literacy, encourage the children to experiment with writing and praise their efforts.

30 Fun Ways to Learn About Writing

More ideas

- Read more books about the alphabet, such as *The Alphabet Tree* by Leo Lionni, *Alphabet Under Construction* by Denise Fleming, *From Anne to Zach* by Mary Jane Martin, *K Is for Kissing a Cool Kangaroo* by Giles Andreae, *The Letters Are Lost!* by Lisa Campbell Ernst, *Mrs. McTats and Her House Full of Cats* by Alyssa Satin Capucilli, *The Vegetable Alphabet Book* by Jerry Pallotta and Bob Thomson, and *What Pete Ate from A to Z* by Maira Kalman.
- Place pads of paper, notebooks, crayons, and markers in various centers throughout the classroom. Encourage the children to use these writing props to enhance their play.
- Make name tags and use them as a transition from one activity to the next. Show the name tags to the children and ask them to pick out their names.

30 Fun Ways to Learn About Writing

3 I Like It!

Discuss what the children like and dislike, and then turn this information into lists with pictures and writing.

Vocabulary

best
clothes
color
favorite
flavor
food
like
love
picture
place
show
smell
sound
taste
toy

What you need

- books about likes and dislikes, such as *Mr. Rabbit and the Lovely Present* by Charlotte Zolotow, *I Only Like What I Like* by Julie Baer, *Peace at Last* by Jill Murphy, and *Bread and Jam for Frances* by Russell Hoban.
- catalogs and magazines
- display board
- food and toy packaging
- paper and blank homemade books
- paper plates
- pens, crayons
- scissors (adult-use only)
- tape or Velcro™
- word bank of themed words (food, toys, places, things, or games)

Learning objectives

Children will:
- Attempt writing for various purposes.
- Know that print and other written language carries meaning and, in English, is read from left to right, top to bottom.
- Use talk to organize, sequence, and clarify thinking, ideas, and feelings.

Before you start

- Cut out photographs and pictures of objects and food from magazines and catalogs. Prepare them for the children to sort and then display by putting tape or a piece of Velcro on the back of each one.

30 Fun Ways to Learn About Writing

- Make a set of two paper plates for each child. Draw a simple happy face and write "Things I like" on one paper plate. Draw a simple sad face and write "Things I do not like" on the second.

What you do

1. Engage the children in a discussion about things they like and things they do not like. Talk about feelings, food, toys, times of day, and places. Be prepared for the children to share some intense feelings.
2. Encourage the children to write about or draw their likes and dislikes.
3. Discuss how what one person likes is not always the same as what another person likes, so we will each make our own list.
4. Read stories about likes and dislikes. (See "What you need" for suggestions.)
5. Ask the children to select pictures of things they like and things they do not like or to draw pictures of their favorite things.
6. Give each child one set of paper plates to use to sort the pictures into "Things I like" and "Things I do not like."

More ideas

- Write the vocabulary words for this activity on a word wall.
- Suggest that the children use a flannel board or Velcro board with food items, figures, and toys to sort their likes and dislikes.

30 Fun Ways to Learn About Writing

4 Bag It!

Words printed on shopping bags are an easy-to-find source of inspiration for children's early writing. Turn part of your art area into a bag factory where the children can personalize bags.

Vocabulary

ad
advertising
bag
brand
buy
company
design
logo
message
sign
slogan
store

What you need

- brushes
- child-safe scissors
- labels for logos
- large, flat surface to work on
- masking tape (to secure bags to the table)
- paint mixed with white glue
- paper or plastic bags with examples of writing and logos
- paper or plastic bags without writing on them
  Note: You can buy plain plastic bags in quantity from a dollar store, or turn used bags inside out.
- waterproof markers in a variety of colors

Learning objectives

Children will:

- Attempt writing for various purposes.
- Know that print and other written language carries meaning.
- Select tools and techniques they need.
- Observe, find out about, and identify features in the place they live.
- Express and communicate their ideas through designs.

What you do

1. Collect some bags from local stores and major chains. Talk with the children about the way pictures and writing are used to convey messages. Ask the children to guess what comes in each bag.

30 Fun Ways to Learn About Writing

child's logo

bags — *masking tape* — *brushes* — *paint mixed with white glue*

❷ Talk about company names and logos that the children recognize, such as McDonalds and Toys "R" Us. What makes them easy to recognize?

❸ Model how you might invent a slogan or a logo for your own name or a store you owned. Help the children make their own logo.

❹ Encourage the children to create their own bags with a logo and writing.

More ideas

- Set up a store in the dramatic play area and make your own bags, signs, and notices.
- Look at ads and signs in newspapers and junk mail.
- Go for a "store walk" in the neighborhood shopping area and look at signs and logos.

30 Fun Ways to Learn About Writing

5 Make a List

This simple activity is easy to set up and can be adapted for a wide range of purposes.

Vocabulary

animals
clothes
colors
drinks
foods
insects
names
toys
vehicles

What you need

- board with examples of lists to support less-confident children
- clipboards (optional)
- examples of lists such as "Shopping List," "My Favorite Things," or "Names"
- pens and pencils
- strips of paper, some stapled into pads

Learning objectives

Children will:

- Attempt writing for a particular purpose.
- Hold and use a pencil effectively to form recognizable letters.
- Read a range of familiar and common words.

Before you start

The children can do this activity inside or outside. You may want to put paper on small clipboards to make it easier for children to make lists while on the move.

What you do

1. Talk about why we need to make lists, and how they help us remember things.
2. Children love collecting names and colors, so start list-making with these categories.

30 Fun Ways to Learn About Writing

❸ Once the concept of list-making is established, change the focus by putting up a sign that will prompt the children to make a list. Suggestions include:
- What do we need to take on the walk to the park?
- How many children have pets?
- Write your name here after you wash your hands.

More ideas

- During group time, brainstorm lists of colors, foods, names, animals, or vehicles. Encourage the children to think of many other categories. Write these lists on chart paper or a white board.
- Make lists of things you will need before outings and events. Write these lists where the children can see you doing it.

30 Fun Ways to Learn About Writing

6 Remember This!

Writing reminders is another way of encouraging children to write with a purpose.

Vocabulary

birthday
bring
dentist
do
doctor
forget
list
need
note
remember
reminder
take

What you need

- calendars and organizers
- *Don't Forget the Bacon* by Pat Hutchins, or another book about remembering
- paper
- pencils and pens
- sticky notes

You might also add

- alarm clock
- birthday book
- board with calendar pages and examples of reminders and lists
- weekly and daily reminder sheets for pictorial and word lists

Learning objectives

Children will:

- Listen with enjoyment and respond to stories.
- Use talk to organize, sequence, and clarify thinking.
- Know that print and other written language carries meaning.
- Attempt writing for various purposes.
- Hold and use a pencil effectively to form recognizable letters.

Before you start

Read the children a story about remembering, such as *Don't Forget the Bacon* by Pat Hutchins.

30 Fun Ways to Learn About Writing

What you do

Weekly class list
November — month
day → 1. 📖 Library day — activity
art → 2. 🎨 November birthdays
3. Recycling!
4. Class pictures

❶ Why is it important to remember things we agreed to do? Talk about things people might forget and need to be reminded about. This could include special occasions such as birthdays; doing regular chores such as taking out the trash or recycling; returning library books and videos; and doctor or dentist appointments.

❷ Talk with the children about things they need to remember and how they can remind themselves. For example, they might need to remember to bring a book to school, to bring their lunch boxes, or to take their coats and papers home.

❸ Tell the children how you help yourself remember things, and demonstrate how you write notes to yourself, or write reminders on a calendar. Encourage the children to help you remember something by asking them to remind you about a letter that needs to be mailed or something you will bring to show them. Talk about how to use a picture, a word, or an object prompt (such as string around your finger) to help you remember things you need to do.

❹ Go through a day or week and help the children make a reminder list, calendar, or set of picture clues.

More ideas

- Ask the children for snack ideas for the next week. Help them write a daily snack list.
- Play a remembering game with the children. Sit in a circle and start the game by saying, "I went to the store and bought an apple." The next child repeats what you said and adds his or her own item to the list, and so on until a child cannot remember the entire list.

30 Fun Ways to Learn About Writing

Make a License Plate

Make some license plates for outside toys or miniature plates for small cars and trucks.

Vocabulary

ambulance
bicycle
book
bus
car
license plate
motorcycle
number names
   from 0–9
trailer
tricycle
truck
uppercase letters
van
vehicle

What you need

- books, pictures, catalogs, and brochures that feature license plates, including car magazines and leaflets
- card stock or poster board
- construction paper
- duct tape or masking tape
- hole punch, string, and child-safe scissors
- large workshop table (you could have this activity outside or near the door)
- markers
- old license plates, if possible
- paper
- pictures or samples of license plates
- stapler
- stickers for little license plates
- white or yellow card stock cut in rectangles

Learning objectives

Children will:

- Link letters and sounds, naming and sounding all the letters of the alphabet.
- Hold and use a pencil effectively to form recognizable letters.

Before you start

Staple pieces of paper together to make a license plate book. Make a cover with construction paper. Staple in place, then cover the staples with masking tape or duct tape.

30 Fun Ways to Learn About Writing

What you do

1. Go for a walk with the children or stand outside and look at license plates. Also look for license plates in books, pictures, catalogs, and brochures. Talk with the children about uppercase letters.
2. Record the license plate numbers the children see in a license plate book.
3. Talk with the children about arrangement of letters and numbers. Look for unusual license plates that say (or almost say) words. Look at the name of the state, and discuss different states' license plates. Talk about license plates from different countries. Can the children find some pictures of them?
4. Depending on what state you live in, you may be able to get some discarded license plates and look at how they are made. Talk about the different colors and pictures on each plate.
5. Help the children use card stock or poster board to make their own license plates with numbers and letters. Attach their plates to wheeled toys and other vehicles, using the hole punch and the string.

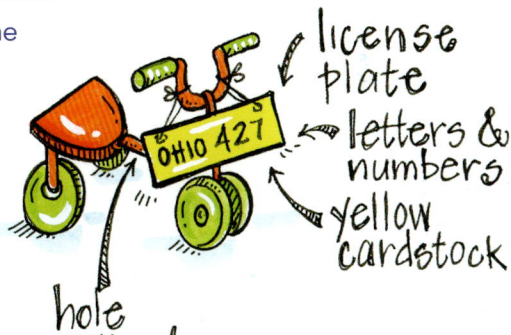

Another idea

- Play a license plate game where the children try to think of a word starting with each letter on the plate.

30 Fun Ways to Learn About Writing

8. Send a Message

Write messages and send them to friends, family, or imaginary characters.

Vocabulary

bottle
letter
message
secret
send/sending/sent
surprise
waterproof

What you need

- bags, envelopes, and small plastic bags
- empty, small plastic containers, with lids
- paper
- pens and pencils
- string or ribbon
- tape

Learning objectives

Children will:

- Know that print and other written language carries meaning.
- Attempt writing for various purposes, using features of different forms.
- Hold and use a pencil effectively to form recognizable letters.
- Use their phonemic knowledge to write simple, familiar words.

What you do

1. Talk with the children about sending messages, including sending secret messages, using messages to surprise people, and saying nice things to people.
2. Talk about places to hide messages so people find them by surprise.
3. Leave a secret message for the children by, for example, tying a note to a balloon, placing a note in a small container in the sand and water table, or hanging a note from a tree or bush.

30 Fun Ways to Learn About Writing

❹ Demonstrate how it is possible to communicate a message with pictures as well as with writing.

❺ Suggest that the children start by creating messages for each other, putting them in empty waterproof containers, and floating them in the water tray.

More ideas

- Collect enough shoeboxes for each child to have a personal message box.
- Display examples of different kinds of messages on the wall of the writing center.

30 Fun Ways to Learn About Writing

9 The Magic Cookbook

Cook up some strange recipes, and make a group cookbook or recipe file.

Vocabulary

add
bake
boil
cook
count
cover
cut
fry
ingredients
measure
mix
pour
recipe
spoon
stir
whisk

What you need

- books about cooking, such as *The Little Red Hen* by Paul Galdone, *Mrs. Greenberg's Messy Hanukkah* by Linda Glaser, *The Little Red Hen Makes a Pizza* by Philemon Sturges, *Cook-a-Doodle-Doo!* by Janet Stevens, *Strega Nona* by Tomie dePaola, or *Oliver's Vegetables* by Vivian French
- card stock or paper for recipes
- cookbooks of all kinds
- glue stick
- pens, crayons
- pictures and clip art of ingredients
- pictures of (and real) cooking tools—for example, whisks, spoons, measuring cups, and pans
- pictures of food

Learning objectives

Children will:

- Explore and experiment with words and texts.
- Begin to understand how information can be found in nonfiction texts.
- Attempt writing for various purposes, using features of different forms such as lists and instructions.

Before you start

Look through magazines and catalogs to find pictures for this activity, or search the Internet for pictures.

30 Fun Ways to Learn About Writing

What you do

1. Use children's experience of cooking in the classroom or at home to talk about food and recipes.
2. Read a book about cooking. (See "What you need" for suggestions.)
3. Look at cookbooks together, and show the children how the books are made up of ingredients and methods. Many cookbooks also have pictures.
4. As a group, create and write a recipe, either real or imaginary. Include a list of ingredients, as well as instructions like measuring, mixing, and counting. Add pictures to the recipe.
5. Talk about some interesting food names, like S'mores and Pigs-in-a-Blanket, and why the foods might have those names.
6. Encourage the children to write their own recipes.

More ideas

- Imagine making a new version of a familiar food—for example, a new yogurt flavor, a new cake, or a new soup.
- Make pictorial recipes by drawing the finished food and labeling the ingredients in the picture.
- Make up a menu for a restaurant for giants or fairies.

30 Fun Ways to Learn About Writing

10 A Toy Story

Use a diary to write and illustrate the real adventures of a stuffed animal or character doll.

Vocabulary

bedtime
car
day
diary
family
food
home
names of the days
   of the week
night
party
plane
sleep
stay
visit

What you need

- bag or small backpack big enough to hold the toy, the diary, and related items
- diary or blank notebook
- luggage tag or label
- postcards and sticky notes
- special pen or pencil
- stuffed animal or doll related to a story, or one from the classroom that the children like

Learning objectives

Children will:
- Use language to imagine and recreate roles and experiences.
- Use their phonetic knowledge to write simple, familiar words.
- Attempt writing for various purposes.
- Know that print and other written language carries meaning and, in English, is read from left to right and top to bottom.

Before you start

Choose an animal or doll to be the main character of this activity.
Attach a label or luggage tag with the name and address of your school on the bag or backpack in case it gets lost!

30 Fun Ways to Learn About Writing

What you do

1. Introduce the character and talk about it. Give it a name and tell its story.
2. Talk with the children and get their ideas about the character: for example, what it likes to eat and where it sleeps.
3. Explain that the children will take turns bringing the toy home and writing in the diary. They can also add postcards and pictures of the things they do together.
4. Make time each day to share what has happened to the toy, where it has been, and what has been written in the diary.
5. During the day, the toy can accompany the children's activities, which they can then record in the diary.
6. Of course, the toy will go on visits, trips, and walks with the class, and may even go on vacation with you or one of the children.

Another idea

- Set up an environment in the classroom for the toy—for example, a bed, a room, or a playground.

30 Fun Ways to Learn About Writing

11 Let's Write About It

You can use any classroom project as a springboard to stimulate children's writing and drawing.

Vocabulary

The vocabulary list will change depending on the project your group is doing.

book
camera
change
day
diary
measure
notebook
picture
record
scrapbook
today
tomorrow
words related to the project you are recording
yesterday

What you need

- books related to the project
- paper and pencils
- pictures, drawings, and word lists
- scrapbooks and diaries
- small, blank homemade books

Learning objectives

Children will:
- Attempt writing for various purposes.
- Hold and use a pencil effectively to form recognizable letters.
- Use their phonetic knowledge to write simple, familiar words.
- Use talk to organize, sequence, and clarify thinking, ideas, feelings, and events.

Before you start

Put a writing area near the center of interest. If possible, hang pictures, children's drawings, and word lists nearby.

What you do

Note: This writing experience can be coordinated with any classroom activity. For example, it can follow a simple activity like taking the children on a walk, having a visitor to the class, or going on a field trip; and, equally well, it can coordinate with a large project like setting up a butterfly box, watching eggs hatch, bringing tadpoles into the classroom, or growing plants and sprouting seeds.

30 Fun Ways to Learn About Writing

❶ You should begin the writing even before you take the walk, start the incubator, or plant the seeds. Encourage the children to anticipate events by making lists and plans, and then to log things as they happen—for example, by measuring plant growth, recording changes in animals, taking pictures, or collecting and labeling items to display.

❷ Model how to write a report of a walk or field trip by doing it together on a flip chart or easel.

❸ Find books, posters, leaflets, and other resources that relate to the activity or project, and discuss them as you add them to a display area.

❹ Share children's writing and other records at group times.

More ideas

- Use a camera to make a visual record of the project.
- Make a scrapbook of pictures, leaflets, and anything else that you collect.
- Keep your own diary and share it with the children.

30 Fun Ways to Learn About Writing

12 Lost and Found

This lost-and-found activity includes making labels and lists. You could organize the lost-and-found box from your school!

Vocabulary

book
describe
description
find
found
"How may I help you?"
label
lose
lost
notice
"What did you lose?"

What you need

- baskets, boxes, or other storage
- book with a lost-and-found theme, such as *Dogger* by Shirley Hughes, or *This Is the Bear* by Sarah Hayes
- card stock, cut for labels
- hole punch, string, and safety pins
- lost-and-found book
- lost-and-found box
- lost-and-found items
- message pad and pens
- old phone (batteries and external cords removed)
- paper for lists and posters

Learning objectives

Children will:

- Use language to imagine and recreate roles and experiences.
- Hold and use a pencil effectively to form recognizable letters.
- Use their phonetic knowledge to write simple, familiar words and make phonetically plausible attempts at more complex words.

Before you start

Look in local papers and post offices or stores for lost-and-found notices to show the children.

30 Fun Ways to Learn About Writing

What you do

1. Begin this activity by reading *Dogger* by Shirley Hughes, *This Is the Bear* by Sarah Hayes, or another book about losing something. Talk to the children about how they might feel if they lost something and then found it. Has this ever happened to them?
2. Set up a lost-and-found prop box in a corner of the room with boxes and labels.
3. Model some activities, such as making a poster to post on telephone poles and bulletin boards, filling in a lost-and-found book with a description of the lost item, writing labels and attaching them to found items, making phone calls to people who have lost items, and responding to callers who are looking for something they lost.
4. Work alongside the children, helping them sort the items and do the activities.
5. Make overnight additions to the "found basket," or leave something of your own outside or in the room to be found.

Another idea

- Has anyone in the class ever visited an animal shelter? Set aside an area in the room for lost pets. This will create many opportunities for writing descriptions, making phone calls, taking messages, and engaging in dramatic play.

30 Fun Ways to Learn About Writing

13 Squishy Bags

Writing in a fun and funky way creates enthusiasm for the mechanics of forming letters.

Vocabulary

alphabet
bag
color
finger
gel
letter
name
squeeze
squirt
squishy
word
write
zipper

What you need

- disposable spoons and cups
- duct tape
- hair gel in fun colors, or plain gel and food coloring
- quart-size zipper-closure bags (1 per child)

Learning objectives

Children will:

- Be confident to try new activities, initiate ideas, and speak in a familiar group.
- Write their names.
- Link letters and sounds.

Before you start

Review the letters of the alphabet with the children. Ask each child to say the first letter of his or her name.

What you do

❶ Give each child a baggie, a spoon, and a disposable cup filled with hair gel.
❷ Ask the children to scoop the hair gel into the baggie until it is about a third full. If using food coloring, let the children squirt a small amount of the color of their choice in the bag.
❸ Help the children squeeze most of the air out of their baggies and securely zip them shut.

30 Fun Ways to Learn About Writing

1. Quart zip bag
2. hair gel
3. food coloring
4. secure with duct tape

bag flat on table

❹ Wipe off the edges of the zippers and secure them with duct tape.
❺ Let the children squish the bags to distribute the food coloring, if needed.
❻ Show the children how to use their fingers as writing utensils to move the gel around in the bag. Can they use their fingers to write letters? Can they write their names?

Another idea

- Bring out the bags whenever the children have to wait for a few moments for others to get ready or to transition from one activity to another. Handling the bags is very soothing.

30 Fun Ways to Learn About Writing

14 Wish You Were Here!

Sending and receiving postcards is good, old-fashioned fun!

Vocabulary

address
buddy
deliver
delivery
letter
letter carrier
mail
mailbox
postcard
post office
send
stamp
vacation
write

What you need

- address book with class addresses
- boxes (optional)
- mailbox
- maps of your area, the country, and the world (optional)
- new blank postcards
- new picture postcards
- pens, crayons, and felt-tip pens
- stamps of the correct amount for a postcard (1 per child)

Learning objectives

Children will:

- Use language to imagine and recreate roles and experiences.
- Attempt writing for various purposes.
- Hold and use a pencil effectively to form recognizable letters.

What you do

1. Ask parents, children, and friends to collect unused postcards for you. Include local scenes, art cards, animals, and people. Talk about why and when we send postcards, and to whom we might send them.
2. Talk about and model the kinds of things someone might want to write on a postcard.
3. Suggest that the children make their own postcards by drawing pictures and writing on the blank cards.

30 Fun Ways to Learn About Writing

❹ Go through your class list and pair up the children. Each child will write a postcard to the other child in the pair.

❺ Show the children how to use the class address book to find the address of their "postcard buddy."

❻ Over the course of the next day or two, help the children write and address their postcards. When they are all finished, put a stamp on each one.

❼ Take a walk to the mailbox and drop them in.

❽ Encourage the children to send postcards back to the class when they go on vacation.

More ideas

- If buying stamps is not possible, or if you have children in your class whose living arrangements make receiving mail at home a problem, do this activity entirely in the classroom. Using a large box, create a classroom mailbox for mailing the postcards, and make individual shoebox mailboxes for each child to receive mail.
- Use a digital camera to make your own postcards with children's pictures or photographs of your school.

30 Fun Ways to Learn About Writing

15 Morning Journals

Having personal journals really helps motivate children to write every day.

Vocabulary

daily
date
habit
journal
notebook
page
writing

What you need

- crayons
- markers
- notebooks, unlined (1 per child)
- pencils
- pens

Learning objectives

Children will:
- Use their phonetic knowledge to write simple, familiar words and make phonetically plausible attempts at more complex words.
- Know that print and other written language carries meaning and, in English, is written and read from left to right and top to bottom.
- Hold and use a pencil effectively to form recognizable letters.

Before you start

If you have old journals of your own with pictures and words, bring them in to show the children.

What you do

❶ Write one child's name on each notebook. Show the children the notebooks and explain that they are their own personal journals to write or draw in.

❷ Explain how to start a journal and tell the children that each day they should start a new page.

30 Fun Ways to Learn About Writing

❸ Establish a "journal time" each morning, or have the journals out on a table for the children to use whenever they wish during the day. The journals are completely personal: the children can write or draw anything that interests them.

❹ Be sure you date each page. Add words to a picture if a child asks for your help.

❺ Keep the journals available all year and send them home with the children at the end of the year. They will be very excited to take their journals home after working on them all year, and it may encourage the wonderful habit of journaling.

Another idea

- Use the journals at the end of the year to help you assess the children's gradual improvement in writing and art skills.

30 Fun Ways to Learn About Writing

16 Secrets and Spies

Secret writing is a fascinating mark-making activity for children. Try experimenting with these different methods.

Vocabulary

cloak
code
dark glasses
disguise
hide
invisible
letter
mask
meet
message
mustache
secret
sneak
whisper
wig

Method 1

What you need

- paper
- very thin paint (blue/black)
- wax candles or white crayons

What to do

- Draw pictures, letters, or patterns on the paper with candles or crayons. Paint over them with thin paint to reveal the messages.

Method 2

What you need

- hair dryer
- lemon juice
- paper and brushes

What to do

- Paint messages with the lemon juice. Heat the paper with a hair dryer to reveal the message.

Learning objectives

Children will:

- Extend their vocabularies, exploring the meanings and sounds of new words.
- Attempt writing for various purposes.
- Use language to imagine and recreate roles and experiences.
- Use talk to organize, sequence, and clarify thinking.

Before you start

Share books or stories with the children about spies and detectives, such as *What Really Happened to Humpty?* by Joe Dumpty as told to Jeanie Franz Ranson or *The Sly Spy (Olivia Sharp: Agent for Secrets)* by Marjorie Weinman Sharmat and Mitchell Sharmat.

30 Fun Ways to Learn About Writing

spy disguise

white crayon

very thin blue paint

What you do

❶ Talk with the children about secret messages and invisible writing. Provide plenty of opportunities for them to explore the methods of secret writing described above.

❷ Talk about spies. Practice sneaking around, whispering, and hiding. What do they think spies might wear, do, and say?

❸ Write secret messages using the methods described.

❹ Provide some spy clothing (hats, wigs, masks, and mustaches) for the children to use as they pretend to be spies.

❺ Model sending a message—for example, by leaving secret messages for the children, asking them to meet you at a special time or in a special place. Arrive in disguise.

More ideas

- Provide carbon paper for experimentation. Children love it!
- Make a "spy camp" in a pop-up tent or other shelter, where children can make secret plans.
- Have a secret message letter box, and encourage the children to put letters in it without being seen.

30 Fun Ways to Learn About Writing

17 So Many Languages

Awaken children to the experience of different languages and alphabets to connect the children to the global community.

Vocabulary

global
globe
good morning
goodbye
hello
language
map
names of different languages and countries
please
thank you
world

What you need

Note: The Internet is a good source of examples of different alphabets, of writing in different languages, of pictures of people from different part of the world, and of restaurant menus in different languages. Your local library will almost certainly have some bilingual books.

- costumes from different countries, particularly those represented in your community (optional)
- dolls in different costumes (optional)
- dual-language picture books
- examples of writing in a range of languages (with translation)
- laminated alphabets in different scripts
- large backing board for posters, pictures, and examples of writing
- newspapers, magazines, and books in various languages
- paper
- pens, pencils, crayons, and markers
- pictures of people from different parts of the world
- restaurant menus from different parts of the world
- world maps and a globe

Dolls
German   Korean

Learning objectives

Children will:
- Know that print and other written language carries meaning.
- Enjoy listening to and using spoken and written language.
- Explore and experiment with sounds, words, and texts.

30 Fun Ways to Learn About Writing

Before you start

Ask the families of the children in your class if there are family members who speak a language other than English. Invite those that do to come to the classroom and share their language with the children. Maybe they could teach a simple song o children's rhyme from their country of origin.

What you do

1. Go for a walk with the children around your neighborhood. Look for writing in different languages.
2. Take pictures of the signs and other writing to create a book for the class.
3. Talk about the languages that people in your community speak.
4. Borrow some dual-language books from your school or local library.
5. Suggest that the children try writing Arabic, Greek, Chinese, or another alphabet with pencils, markers, or brushes and black paint.
6. Learn how to say "Hello, "Goodbye," "Please," and "Thank you," in other languages, then teach the children how to say and to write these words.

More ideas

- Write bilingual labels and instructions in a language that is meaningful to the children in your class.
- Find one or two picture dictionaries in languages other than English, and learn how to say and write some of the words.

30 Fun Ways to Learn About Writing

18 Long, Long Ago

Explore how people wrote long, long ago. Experiment with quill pens, scrolls, and homemade ink.

Vocabulary

blotting paper
century
dip
envelope
feather
greetings
ink
nib
penknife
quill
scroll

What you need

- blotting paper
- feathers to use as quills (available from school supply stores and catalogs and from craft and hobby stores)
- paper torn at the edges rather than cut
- paper washed with diluted coffee to make it look old
- pictures or copies of old documents
- rolls of paper and ribbon
- washable ink or "ink" made from diluted watercolor paint—offer brown and blue as well as black
- waterproof covering for the table, and then a cloth on top

Learning objectives

Children will:
- Attempt writing for various purposes.
- Hold and use a writing implement effectively to form recognizable letters.
- Find out about the past.

What you do

1. Show the children the feathers. Talk about how people used to use them to write. Show a picture of this, and model how to hold the feather. You can cut them to a nib shape if you want.

   Note: Information about writing with a feather, how to hold a feather, and how to cut a nib shape in a feather are readily available on the Internet. Try searching under "How to make a quill pen."

30 Fun Ways to Learn About Writing

Illustration labels: feather; end; ① cut end at an angle; ② end will look like this; washable ink (diluted watercolor)

② Set out the quills and small containers of washable ink. Show the children how to dip the end of the quill into the ink.

❸ Encourage free exploration of the materials. Help the children write on different types of paper.

❹ Offer different colors of paper and ink, if desired.

❺ Talk about blotting paper and model how to use it.

❻ Talk about the language used in old-fashioned letters. Encourage the children to write an old-fashioned letter, perhaps to a family member.

❼ Show the children how to roll up a letter and fasten it with ribbon.

More ideas

- Visit a museum to look at old-fashioned writing. Find a picture of the Declaration of Independence for the children to study.
- Make a special scroll with all the children's names on it. Display the scroll in the classroom.
- Make your own envelopes and use sealing wax to seal them. (You can improvise sealing wax by using the drip from a colored candle.)
  Safety note: When using sealing wax or a candle, keep the children well away from the flame.

30 Fun Ways to Learn About Writing

19 Signs of Writing

Take a walk and look for signs and notices before you set up this writing area. Remember to take a camera with you.

Vocabulary

accident
car
careful
circle
construction
hexagon
names of colors
rectangle
sign
square
slow
stop
traffic
triangle
vehicle
warning

What you need

- card stock cut in rectangles, hexagons, circles, and triangles
- child-safe scissors
- craft sticks
- crayons
- glue
- markers
- paint and paintbrushes
- pencils and pens
- photographs and other pictures of signs—for example, road signs, street signs, directions, store signs, notices, and warnings

  Note: If you do not find enough to photograph in your immediate neighborhood, use a search engine to find more on the Internet.
- toy people and vehicles

Learning objectives

Children will:

- Attempt writing for various purposes.
- Use talk to organize, sequence, and clarify thinking and ideas.
- Observe, find out about, and identify features of the neighborhood where they go to school.
- Read a range of familiar and common words.

What you do

❶ With the children, take a walk in your neighborhood to look for construction signs, traffic signs, and road signs.

30 Fun Ways to Learn About Writing

– signs –

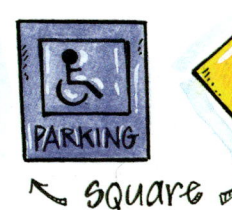

triangle ← square → circle rectangle hexagon

IN OUT House for rent EXIT Yard sale

– other signs –

❷ Talk about signs and notices that the children know, and their purposes and meanings.

❸ Talk about the shapes and colors of different signs—for example, yellow triangles, red hexagons.

❹ When you are back in the classroom, use toy people and vehicles to practice what happens when drivers and pedestrians see different signs.

❺ Encourage the children to make signs, with appropriate symbols and colors, to use with the toy people and vehicles. Create situations such as ordinary driving, road work, police events, and accidents.

More ideas

- Together, make some large signs for the playground, the classroom, or the whole building.
- Make some picture or symbol signs.
- Make dual-language signs.
- Look in catalogs and magazines for pictures of signs. The children can cut them out and make a scrapbook.

30 Fun Ways to Learn About Writing

20 Let's Go on a Visit!

Before you go on a walk, visit, or other excursion, use the planning and anticipation as a stimulus for writing.

Vocabulary

backpack
bus
camera
jacket
lunch
map
name of the place you are visiting
picnic
relevant vocabulary, such as the names of zoo animals or beach words
sandwiches
ticket
visit
water bottle

What you need

- backpack or other bag with the things you need to bring
- leaflets, pictures, and descriptions of the place you are visiting
- maps of the area
- notebooks to record things you want to remember
- pens, pencils, and crayons
- photographs and pictures of the things you need (optional)
- strips of paper for lists

Learning objectives

Children will:

- Interact with others, negotiating plans and activities.
- Extend their vocabularies.
- Use talk to organize, sequence, and clarify thinking and ideas.
- Attempt writing for various purposes, such as lists and stories.
- Hold and use a pencil effectively to form recognizable letters.

What you do

❶ Talk with the children about where you are taking the class for a visit. Allow time for anticipation and planning. Discuss when and where you are going. Talk about what you will see and learn.

❷ Talk through the sequence of planning for a trip.

❸ Look at maps, plans, and pictures together.

❹ Talk about lists and reminders, and model how to write and use them.

30 Fun Ways to Learn About Writing

Illustration labels: backpack, sweater inside, notebook, water, pencil & markers, map, Famer's Market, pumpkins, apples, corn, apple cider, pumpkin painting today

Before the trip: "I want to paint my own pumpkin" / "I want to drink some apple cider!"

After the trip: "I saw lots and lots of funny pumpkins." / "I saw different color apples!"

5 Ask the children to suggest what you need to take, collect, and learn before you go.

6 Use travel guides and information leaflets to help the children with prediction and planning—for example, "What if…?" and "What do we need for…?"

7 Encourage the children to write or dictate a few words about what they are most interested in seeing or doing on the trip. Save what the children wrote and then ask them to write about what they saw on the trip. What did they most enjoy? What was most interesting?

More ideas

- Use toy people to stimulate talk about the visit and to "walk through" the sequence of events in advance.
- Use the opportunity to make tickets, build with blocks, and make big maps outside with playground chalk.

30 Fun Ways to Learn About Writing

21 Going My Way?

Making maps and following them provides lots of opportunity for writing and organizing words and drawing.

Vocabulary

This list will vary according to your specific situation.

alternate
corner
crosswalk
direction/directions
home
library
map
park
parking lot
road
route
school
start
street
traffic light
travel

What you need

- aerial photographs (optional)
  Note: Aerial photographs are available on the Internet.
- large sheets of paper
- pens, pencils, markers, and crayons
- road maps, floor plans, and other "bird's eye views"
- street maps and maps of your local area

Learning objectives

Children will:
- Attempt writing for various purposes.
- Use language to imagine and recreate roles and experiences.
- Use talk to organize, sequence, and clarify thinking and ideas.
- Observe, find out about, and identify features in the place they live.

Before you start

Display maps (and aerial photographs, if possible) on the wall.

What you do

❶ Make sure there is room for big sheets of paper and for two or three children to work together. You could push two tables together or make this a floor activity.

❷ Start by looking at some maps and talking with the children about the maps' features.

❸ Encourage the children to make maps of their journeys between home and school.

30 Fun Ways to Learn About Writing

child's map

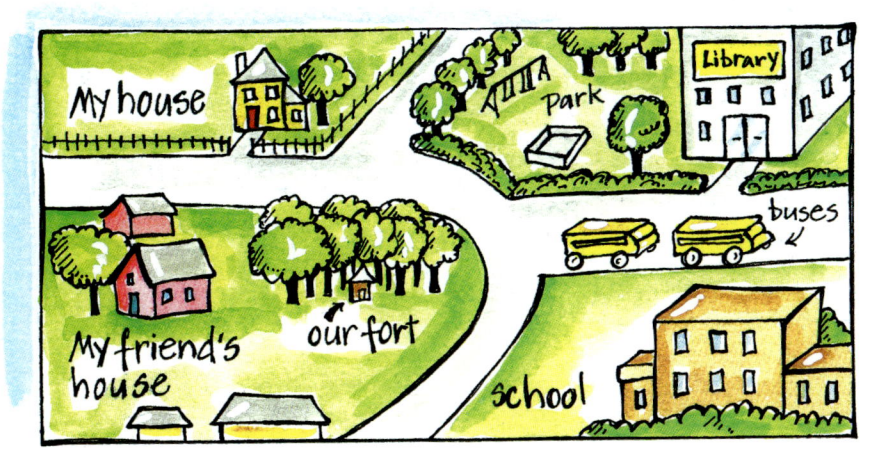

4. Talk through the journeys as the children draw their maps. Encourage them to add pictures of the features and landmarks they pass each day. (Store, church, library, firehouse, and so on).
5. As they work, encourage the children to describe their journeys to the other children.
6. When the children complete these maps and plans, ask the children to show you the route between two places on their maps—for example, from the school to the library.
7. When individual children are ready, ask them to write or dictate the directions for the routes they drew.

Another idea

- Make a huge map of the classroom, or the school grounds, or the neighborhood, on a large piece of paper or in chalk on the floor or outside.

30 Fun Ways to Learn About Writing

22 In Character

Link writing to a book or story that the children know and love. Have dress-up clothes ready for the writers to get into character.

Vocabulary

This list will vary according to your specific situation.

- colors
- food item lists
- ingredients
- items linked to the story
- lists of characters
- places from the story

What you need

- paper of different kinds, sizes, and colors
- pens, pencils, crayons, and markers
- stickers, stamps, and other decorative items
- suggestions for characters and costumes, for example:
  - apron for "The Little Red Hen" (writing recipes)
  - crowns for a royal story (writing proclamations/laws)
  - giant pens and paper (writing a giant letter)
  - Red Riding Hood cloak (writing shopping lists)
  - teddy bear hat (letters to Goldilocks or porridge recipes)
  - wizards' hats (writing spells)

Learning objectives

Children will:
- Use language to imagine and recreate roles and experiences.
- Retell narratives in the correct sequence.
- Attempt writing for various purposes.
- Show an understanding of the elements of a story, such as the main character and the sequence of events.

Before you start

Choose a story with a character that the children like.

What you do

❶ Decorate the classroom with pictures and photographs that relate to the story or book, or to the characters in the story or book.

30 Fun Ways to Learn About Writing

apron *recipe*
Little Red Hen

cloak *basket*
Little Red Riding Hood

crown *shoe* *pillow*
Cinderella

sticks *straw* *bricks* *paper houses* *wolf mask*
The Three Little Pigs

❷ Read or tell the story and talk about the main character and how that character might talk, walk, behave, and eat.

❸ Practice walking like a giant, a king, a hen, a bear, and other characters stories mention.

❹ Talk about the kind of writing the character might do. For example, would the character write a list, a letter, a recipe?

❺ Brainstorm suitable writing implements for a giant, a bear, a fairy, or the character in the story. Decide what kind of paper the character might use.

❻ Give the children time for free play with the props you have collected, as well as time to draw or write as they think the character in the story would.

More ideas

- Make a giant book of giant letters.
- Use circle time for the children to share their writings with each other.

30 Fun Ways to Learn About Writing

55

23 Seeds "R" Us

Use beans, peas, and other dried seeds to make a seed store or a garden center.

Vocabulary

beans
catalog
color
envelope
flower
grow
list
money
packet
pay
peas
plant
price
receipt
seed
small

What you need

- empty envelopes or small plastic bags
- gardening magazines
- green jackets (you can dye old white shirts) with name badges
- labels and stickers for badges and seed envelopes
- paper for lists
- seed catalogs
- seed packets
- variety of loose seeds

Learning objectives

Children will:
- Observe, find out about and identify some features of living things, objects, and events.
- Know that print and other written language carries meaning.
- Hold and use a pencil effectively to form recognizable letters.

Before you start

Your local garden center may have posters and other brochures and notices to enhance this activity.

What you do

❶ If possible, visit a garden center with the children.
❷ Collect gardening brochures, seed catalogs, magazines, and seed packets.

30 Fun Ways to Learn About Writing

(dyed shirt) — green jacket
catalogs
seeds
paper and markers
Seed Store sign
envelopes
zip bags
labels & stickers

← add child's name
← badge

❸ You could work as a class to write letters requesting catalogs, or call a few companies for seed and bulb catalogs.

❹ Look carefully at the seed packets, noting the pictures of seeds and plants on them. Point out the growing instructions printed on the back.

❺ Get out the envelopes, plastic bags, and seeds for the children to make into seed packets.

❻ Model the activity of decorating and filling the packets. Help as needed with writing or drawing the growing instructions.

❼ Together, write and illustrate a list of the different kinds of seeds for sale.

❽ Now, set up a store for selling the seed packets.

❾ Have the children make and decorate a sign for their seed store.

❿ Encourage dramatic play in the store, using the green shirts for uniforms and adding writing materials for lists, bills, and receipts.

More ideas

- Try actually growing some of the seeds. Each day, ask one child to draw or write in a class book what happens as the seeds grow.
- As an alternative, each child could keep his own plant diary, recording his observations in whatever way he wishes.
- Sing the song, "Oats, Peas, Beans, and Barley Grow" at circle time.

30 Fun Ways to Learn About Writing

24 Going to the Hospital

Doctors and nurses take care of patients and keep records of accidents, injuries, and treatments.

Vocabulary

accident
ambulance
bandage
better
broken
cast
doctor
hospital
nurse
patient
record
stethoscope
stretcher
temperature
thermometer
wheelchair
worse
X-ray

What you need

- books about hospitals (see "What you do" for suggestions)
- clipboards and paper
- pens
- shoebox, for a filing cabinet
- teddy bears or other stuffed animals
- toy or discarded cell phones (batteries removed)
- toy first-aid box
- toy stethoscopes
- toy thermometers
- X-rays, pretend or real

Learning objectives

Children will:

- Interact with others, negotiating plans and activities, and taking turns in conversations.
- Attempt writing for various purposes.
- Use language to imagine and recreate roles and experiences.
- Use talk to organize, sequence, and clarify thinking, ideas, and feelings.

Before you start

Go to the library and check out books about going to the hospital. Some suggestions are listed below. Visit your local hospital for leaflets and brochures that you can share with the children.

30 Fun Ways to Learn About Writing

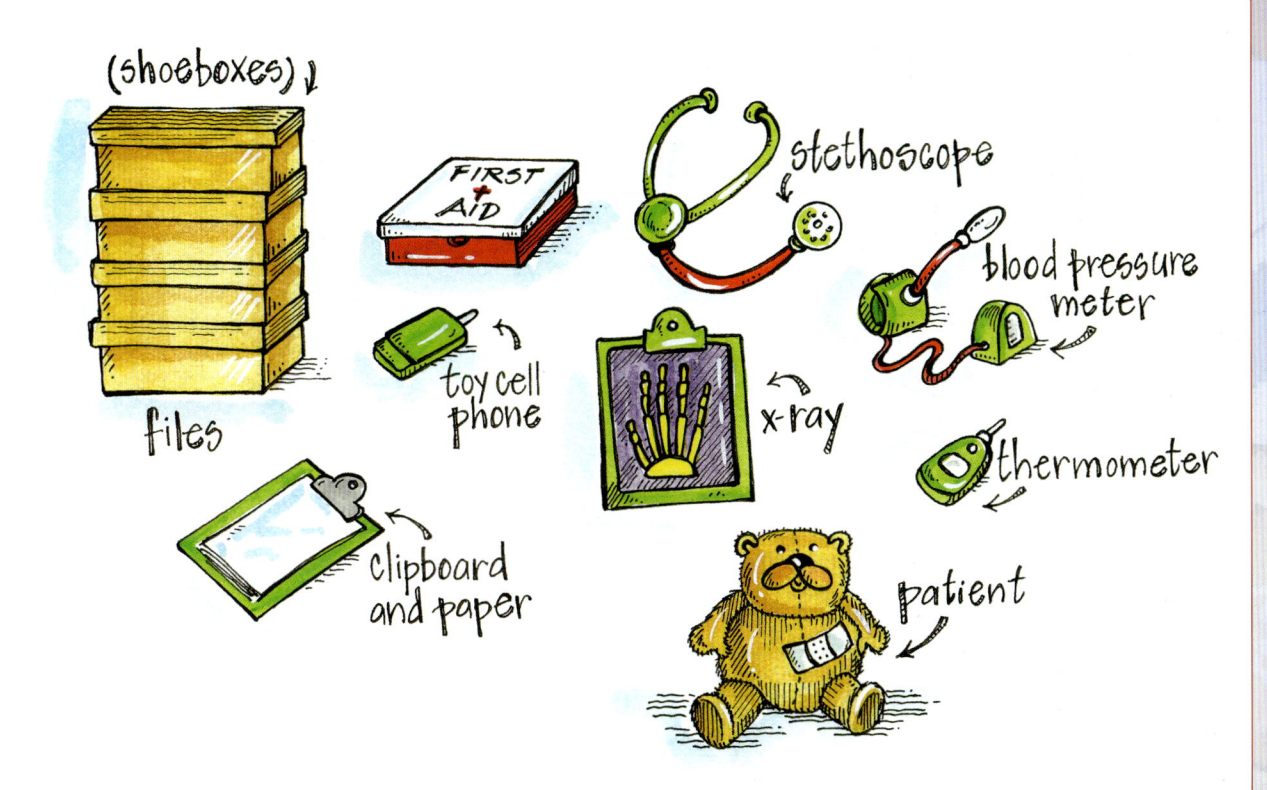

(shoeboxes)
files
FIRST AID
toy cell phone
stethoscope
x-ray
blood pressure meter
thermometer
clipboard and paper
patient

What you do

❶ Talk about what happens when you are hurt or have an accident. What about if you are very, very sick? Ask the children to contribute their experiences.

❷ Look at books about hospitals, such as *Do I Have to Go to the Hospital?* by Pat Thomas, *Good-Bye Tonsils!* by Juliana Lee Hatkoff, or *What's Inside a Hospital?* by Sharon Gordon.

❸ Talk about what doctors and nurses do.

❹ Use dolls or teddy bears as patients. Encourage the children to write records and reports of their patients' treatment and progress.

More ideas

- Make one of the wheeled toys into an ambulance that can take patients to the "hospital" in the classroom.
- Make medical record cards for the patients.
- Encourage the children to create an animal hospital where they can be veterinarians with stuffed animals as patients.

30 Fun Ways to Learn About Writing

25 Fire, Fire!

A firefighter's hat, a phone, and a notebook create exciting writing opportunities.

Vocabulary

911
address
ambulance
coming
danger
fire
help
hospital
ladder
message
number
police
quickly
rescue
stairs
window

What you need

- bell to ring for an alarm
- clipboards, paper, and notebooks
- firefighter's hat, police helmet
- pens and pencils
- phone book and street map
- pictures of rescue services
- sticky notes
- toy telephone, cell phone, or pager

Learning objectives

Children will:
- Be attentive listeners, responding to what they have heard with appropriate actions.
- Speak clearly and audibly with confidence and control.
- Attempt writing for various purposes.
- Hold and use a pencil effectively to form recognizable letters.
- Use language to imagine and recreate roles and experiences.

Before you start

Prepare a script of a person calling 911 about an emergency.

What you do

❶ Take your class to visit a fire station and ask if you can look at the office or ask a firefighter to explain what happens in the office.

30 Fun Ways to Learn About Writing

❷ Back in the classroom, model taking an emergency call and noting the number.

❸ Talk about emergencies—what they are, how you feel, what you do, and who can help. Talk about all kinds of situations where someone might need quick help, such as being locked out of one's home, a baby being born, someone who is very sick, animal rescues, accidents, and fires.
Note: There may be a child in your group who has experienced an actual emergency involving the police or the fire department. Be sure to allow safe space for such a child to talk if she wishes.

❹ Look at a local map, and mark the children's homes and the school on the map.

❺ Show the children how to make an emergency call.

❻ Discuss the importance of 911 calls, when to make a 911 call, and the importance of remembering the number in case you need it.

❼ Work in pairs: one child calls about an emergency while the other one writes the message.

Another idea

- Link this activity with inside or outside dramatic play, using helmets, vehicles, and dolls or puppets.

30 Fun Ways to Learn About Writing

26 May I Take a Message?

Using the telephone is at the center of this activity. Providing message pads and pens will make it more realistic.

Vocabulary

answer
at work
busy
call back
"How may I help you?"
"Just a moment, please."
"May I take a message?"
"May I ask who is calling?"
meeting
message
number
out
talk
write

What you need

- digital camera and printer
- message pads and clipboards
- pens and pencils
- phone books and directories
- phones (wall mounted, desk, cordless, and cell)
- sticky notes

Learning objectives

Children will:

- Interact with others, negotiating plans and activities, and taking turns in conversations.
- Speak clearly and audibly with confidence and control.
- Attempt writing for various purposes.
- Hold and use a pencil effectively to form recognizable letters.

Before you start

Remove batteries from cell phones and cordless phones, and remove any external wires from the traditional phones. Clean phones with antiseptic wipes or spray. Use a digital camera to take pictures of all the children and the teachers in the class. Print out the pictures and hang them on the wall.

What you do

❶ Look at the different kinds of phones.

30 Fun Ways to Learn About Writing

digital photos
clip board
message

cell phone

cordless phone

wall-mounted phone

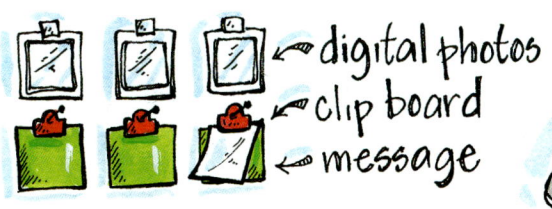

desk phone

❷ Visit the school office or other offices to watch how people answer the phone and take messages. What kind of phones do they use in the office? What kinds of phones do the children have at home?

❸ Model answering the phone yourself. Take messages and make notes.

❹ Encourage the children to explore the phones before introducing more formal activities.

❺ Hang pictures of children, staff, and other adults on the wall, and hang clips underneath each for messages.

❻ Depending on the ages of your children, you might model looking up numbers in a phone book or directory. If you have older children and a classroom computer, you could demonstrate how to look up a phone number on the Internet.

❼ Talk about how to leave a message and how to take a message. Help the children take phone messages.

More ideas

- Discuss alphabetical order; display an alphabet chart to help with the concept. When you hang the pictures of the children, hang them in alphabetical order by first name.
- Make message sheets on a computer and let the children suggest what these sheets need to look like and contain.

30 Fun Ways to Learn About Writing

27 Staying at a Hotel

Turn your housekeeping area into a hotel or bed and breakfast. Then set up a check-in desk to encourage children's writing.

Vocabulary

balcony
bathroom
bedroom
bills
credit card
elevator
"How long are you staying?"
key
luggage
pool
reception
restaurant
"Sign here, please."

What you need

- calculator or old adding machine
- calendar or organizer
- hotel brochures
- keys with tags or old swipe cards
- message pad and pens
- paper and envelopes
- phone
- travel leaflets

Learning objectives

Children will:

- Use language to imagine and recreate roles and experiences.
- Extend their vocabularies, exploring the meanings and sounds of new words.
- Attempt writing for various purposes.
- Hold and use a pencil effectively to form recognizable letters.

Before you start

You can collect leaflets of local attractions from most hotel lobbies, even if you are not staying there!

What you do

❶ Give the children time to talk about what it is like to stay in a hotel or a bed and breakfast. Tell about your own experiences.

Note: If there are children in your class who do not have experience with hotels, be sure to read books about hotels, such as *Olivia and the Haunted*

30 Fun Ways to Learn About Writing

Hotel by Jodie Shepherd, *Weekend at the Grand Hotel* by Mary Labatt, *Pip in the Gran Hotel* by Johannes Hucke, or *Eloise* by Kay Thompson. This will give everyone some common ground for play and conversation.

❷ Try to arrange a class visit to a hotel. Make arrangements in advance! Maybe you and the children can take a tour of the building. You might see the lobby, guest rooms, a laundry room, or a janitorial area. Look around and notice what people are doing. Talk about what you saw when you get back to the classroom.

❸ Talk through the sequence of checking in to a hotel.

❹ Model some hotel activities, verbal and written, such as calling to make a reservation, taking information from a guest over the phone, welcoming a guest, filling in forms, signing in, finding keys, writing bills, and paying for your stay.

❺ Practice taking calls and messages and having telephone conversations.

❻ Help the children use writing or drawing to create labels, lists, memos, and messages.

Another idea

- Set up a hotel restaurant, write a menu, and take orders for meals.

30 Fun Ways to Learn About Writing

28 Ticket, Please!

Children love making and using tickets. Give them a format and a place to work, and they will be off!

Vocabulary

adult
agent
airplane
child
concert
cost
date
family
half-price
movie
museum
pay
price
seat number
show
ticket
time
train
zoo

What you need

- child-safe scissors (plain and with patterned edges)
- hole punch
- stapler
- sample forms and tickets
- pens and other markers
- pieces of card stock in different sizes and colors
- rolls of paper (adding machine rolls)
- stamps with pictures and designs

Learning objectives

Children will:

- Interact with others, negotiating plans and activities.
- Use language to imagine and recreate roles and experiences.
- Attempt writing for various purposes.

What you do

1. Collect a variety of used tickets; ask families and children to contribute to the collection. Make a scrapbook for reference. Collect tickets from buses and trains, airplanes, concerts, movies, museums, zoos, shows, and raffles.
2. Talk about why you need tickets. What is on a ticket? Look at your collection and note similarities and differences. Look at dates, times, prices, half-price information, children's tickets, pictures, and designs.

30 Fun Ways to Learn About Writing

Labels on illustration: number, tickets, Children's Theater, May 21, date, hole punch, stapler, paper clips, stamps, roll of paper, cardstock, scissors (with patterned edges), phone

❸ Introduce the children to the ticket-making area and talk about what it offers. Let the children play freely, then help them make their own tickets if they ask for help.

❹ The children will need little encouragement to incorporate ticket-making into their dramatic play.

More ideas

- Use a large appliance box with a window cut into the side (adult step only) to make a ticket office or a box office. Add a small table and chair inside the "office" for the ticket agent.
- Have a concert, show, or exhibition and make the tickets for it.

30 Fun Ways to Learn About Writing

29 When Can You Come?

Link making appointments and writing in appointment books to a hair salon or barber shop.

Vocabulary

appointment
blow dry
cut
haircut
long
names of the days of the week
next (next week, next appointment, "Who's next?")
permanent
rollers
shampoo
short/shorter
straighten
time
wash
"What time?"
"When can you come?"

What you need

- appointment book
- appointment cards
- calendar or organizer
- clock
- magazines
- old cell phones, batteries removed
- pens and erasers
- style books with different hairstyles for adults and children

Learning objectives

Children will:

- Use language to imagine and recreate roles and experiences.
- Interact with others, negotiating plans and activities, and taking turns in conversations.
- Speak clearly and audibly with confidence and control.
- Hold and use a pencil effectively to form recognizable letters.

What you do

1. Visit a local hair salon or barber shop, if possible.
2. Talk about what it means to make an appointment.
3. Model what you say and what the person at the shop says.
4. Talk about appointment books and how to use them.

30 Fun Ways to Learn About Writing

appointment card

clock

appointment book

pens & eraser

organizer

calculator

old cell phone

magazines

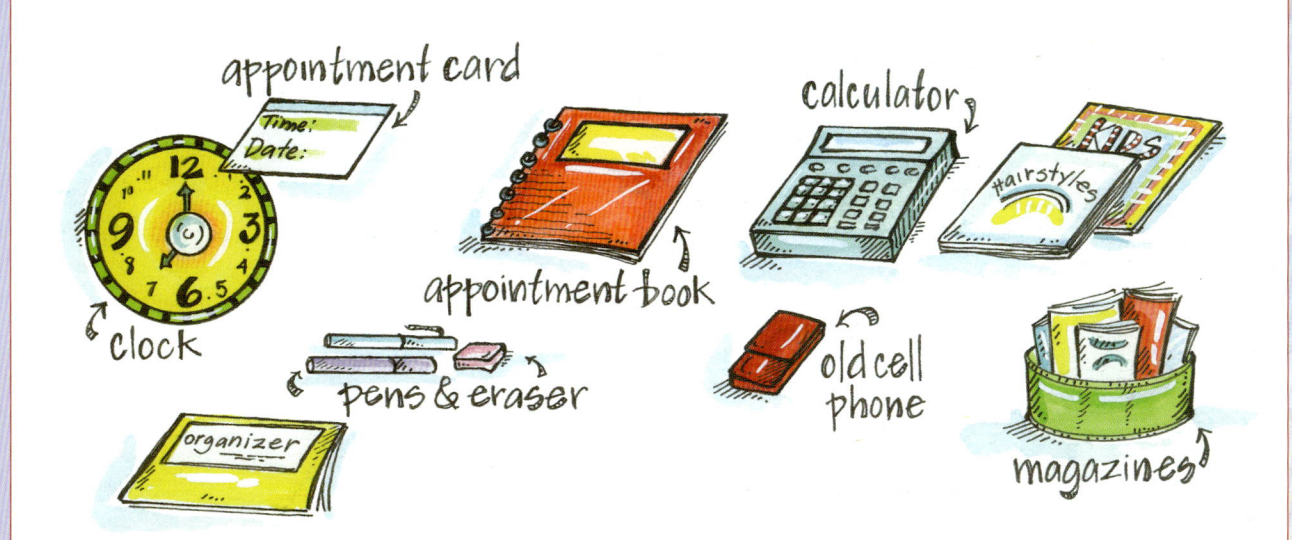

❺ Give the children plenty of time for free play before suggesting a direction.

❻ Write the special words for this activity on a word wall.

❼ Help the children make appointment cards and talk to them about reminders.

❽ Encourage the children to write price lists and make appointments for children and parents.

More ideas

- Create a hair salon with a waiting room and a long table for the stylists. Have plenty of mirrors.
- Make a hairstyle book with digital photographs of the children and their families.

30 Fun Ways to Learn About Writing

30 RSVP

Plan an event, and then offer materials for the children to write planning lists and invitations.

Vocabulary

celebration
date
family
invitation
invite
party
reply
RSVP
send
starts
time
write
"You are invited…"

What you need

- sample invitations
- colored paper
- envelopes
- glue or glue sticks
- list of names of the people to invite
- patterned paper
- pencils or pens
- sequins, glitter, and stickers
- streamers and balloons (optional)
- thin card stock in mixed colors

Learning objectives

Children will:

- Interact with others, negotiating plans and activities, and taking turns in conversations.
- Attempt writing for various purposes.
- Know that print and other written language carries meaning and, in English, is read from left to right and top to bottom.
- Hold and use a pencil effectively to form recognizable letters.

What you do

1. Talk about celebrations and the kinds of things people celebrate.
2. Choose an event to celebrate in the classroom. It might be a seasonal celebration, the completion of a class project, or a program the children have prepared for families or for another class.

30 Fun Ways to Learn About Writing

Illustration labels: invitations, balloons, colored paper, patterned paper, envelopes, glitter, sequins, stickers, list of adults & children

❸ Decide what will happen at the celebration. Make lists of what you will need—food, games, seating, decorations, songs, and anything else the class thinks is necessary.

❹ Make a list of the people to invite to the celebration or event.

❺ Talk about invitations and how they are worded. Look at some commercially produced invitations and the signs and symbols they use—for example, bells and rings for weddings, and balloons and candles for birthdays.

❻ Help the children create their own invitations to their event.

More ideas

- Encourage the children to invite each other to events and parties in the dramatic play area.
- Make invitations and have parties for dolls and stuffed animals.

Index

A

Adding machine rolls, 66
Adding machines, 64
Address books, 38
Alarm clocks, 22
Alike and different, 12
Alphabet charts, 63
Alphabetical order, 63
Anticipating, 33, 50–51
Antiseptic wipes, 62
Appliance boxes, 67
Appointment books, 8, 12, 68
Appointment cards, 68
Aprons, 54
Assessment, 41

B

Backpacks, 30, 50
Bags, 26, 30, 50
    paper, 18
    plastic, 18, 26, 56
    shopping, 18
    zipper-close, 36
Balloons, 26, 70
Bathroom scales, 12
Bells, 60
Birthday books, 12, 22
Blank books, 12, 16, 32
Block graphs, 17
Blotting paper, 46
Body awareness, 12–13
Books, 24, 32–33
    The Alphabet Tree by Leo Lionni, 15

Alphabet Under Construction by Denise Fleming, 15
Bread and Jam for Francis by Russell Hoban, 16
Chicka Chicka Boom Boom by Bill Martin Jr. & John Archambault, 14
Cook-a-Doodle-Doo! by Janet Stevens, 28
Do I Have to Go to the Hospital? by Pat Thomas, 59
Dogger by Shirley Hughes, 34–35
Don't Forget the Bacon by Pat Hutchins, 22
Eloise by Kay Thompson, 65
From Anne to Zach by Mary Jane Martin, 15
Good-Bye Tonsils! by Juliana Lee Hatkoff, 59
I Only Like What I Like by Julie Baer, 16
K Is for Kissing a Cool Kangaroo by Giles Andreae, 15
The Letters Are Lost! by Lisa Campbell Ernst, 15
The Little Red Hen by Paul Galdone, 28
The Little Red Hen Makes a Pizza by Philemon Sturges, 28
Mr. Rabbit and the Lovely Present by Charlotte Zolotow, 16
Mrs. Greenberg's Messy Hanukkah by Linda Glaser, 28
Mrs. McTats and Her House Full of Cats by Alyssa Satin Capucilli, 15
Oliver's Vegetables by Vivian French, 28
Olivia and the Haunted Hotel by Jodie Shepherd, 65
Peace at Last by Jill Murphy, 16
Pip in the Gran Hotel by Johannes Hucke, 65

30 Fun Ways to Learn About Writing

The Sly Spy (Olivia Sharp: Agent for Secrets) by Marjorie Weinman Sharmat & Mitchell Sharmat, 42
Strega Nona by Tomie dePaola, 28
This Is the Bear by Sarah Hayes, 34–35
The Vegetable Alphabet Book by Jerry Pallotta & Bob Thomson, 15
Weekend at the Grand Hotel by Mary Labatt, 65
What Pete Ate from A to Z by Maira Kalman, 15
What Really Happened to Humpty? by Joe Dumpty by Jeanie Franz Ranson, 42
What's Inside a Hospital? by Sharon Gordan, 59
Boxes, 34, 38–39, 43
    appliance, 67
    first-aid, 58
    shoeboxes, 27, 39, 58
Brainstorming, 21
Brochures, 24, 56, 64

C

Calculators, 64
Calendars, 12, 22–23, 64, 68
Cameras, 13, 33, 39, 45, 48, 62
Candles, 42, 47
Carbon paper, 43
Card stock, 24, 28, 34, 48, 66, 70
Catalogs, 16, 24, 28, 49
Chalk, 51, 53
Chart paper, 21
Charts, 8, 12
Circle time, 55, 57
Clarifying thinking, 9, 16–17, 22–23, 32, 42–43, 48–53, 58–59
Class books, 57
Clip art, 28

Clipboards, 8, 13, 17, 20, 58, 60, 62
Cloaks, 54
Clocks, 68
    alarm, 22
Coffee, 46
Communicating through design, 18–19
Computer labels, 14
Computers, 8, 44, 52, 63
Construction paper, 24
Cookbooks, 8, 28–29
Cooperation, 8, 50–51, 58–59, 62–63, 66–67, 70–71
Costumes, 44
Craft sticks, 48
Crayons, 15–16, 28, 38, 40, 42, 44, 50, 52, 54
Creative development, 9, 34, 38–39, 42–43, 52–55, 58–61, 64–71
Crowns, 54
Cultural diversity, 12, 44–45
Cups
    measuring, 28
    plastic, 36
Curiosity, 7

D

Decoding symbols, 7
Descriptive language, 12–13, 53
Diaries, 12, 30, 32, 57
Display boards, 12, 16, 22, 44
Dolls, 30, 44, 61, 71
Dramatic play, 8, 19, 35, 54–61, 64–71
Drawings, 32
Dress-up clothes, 43, 54–55
Dual-language books, 44–45
Duct tape, 24, 36

E

Easels, 33

30 Fun Ways to Learn About Writing

Emergent writing, 7
Emotional development, 8
Envelopes, 8, 26, 47, 56, 64, 70
Environmental print, 7
Erasers, 68

F
Feathers, 46
Felt-tip pens, 38
Field trips, 32–33
    barber shop, 68
    fire station, 60
    hair salon, 68
    hotel, 65
    museums, 47
    shopping center, 19
Fine motor skills, 7, 9, 12, 14–15, 20–27, 32–35, 38–41, 46–47, 50–51, 56–57, 62–65, 68–71
Firefighter hats, 60
First-aid boxes, 58
Flannel boards, 17
Flip charts, 13, 33
Floor plans, 52
Food coloring, 36
Food packaging, 16
Forms, 8, 66
Free play, 7, 47, 55, 67, 69

G
Gardening activities, 57
Glitter, 70
Globes, 44
Glue, 18, 48, 70
    sticks, 28, 70
Greeting cards, 12
Gross motor skills, 13

H
Hair dryers, 42
Hair gel, 36
Hand-eye coordination, 7
Handwriting, 8
Hats, 43
    firefighter, 60
    police helmets, 60
    teddy bear, 54
    wizard, 54
History, 46–47
Hole punches, 24, 34, 66

I
Imitation, 7
Independence, 8
Invitations, 70

J
Jackets, 56
Journals, 40–41
Junk mail, 8, 19

K
Keys, 64

L
Labels, 8, 18, 30, 34, 56
    bilingual, 45
Laminated alphabets, 44
Language diversity, 8, 44–45, 49
Leaflets, 24, 33, 50–51, 64
Lemon juice, 42
Letter recognition, 9, 14, 20–25, 32–41, 46–47, 50–51, 55–57, 60–65, 68–71
License plates, 24
Listening skills, 7–8, 22–23, 44–45, 60
Lists, 8–9, 12, 16, 20, 23, 28, 32, 50, 56–57, 65, 69–70

30 Fun Ways to Learn About Writing

Literacy skills, 7–9, 20–21, 48–49
Logos, 19
Lost-and-found items, 34
Luggage tags, 30

M

Magazines, 8, 16, 24, 28, 44, 49, 56, 68
Mailboxes, 38
Maps, 38, 44, 50–53, 60
Markers, 14–15, 24, 40, 44, 48, 52, 54, 66
    waterproof, 18
Masking tape, 18, 24
Masks, 43
Measuring cups, 28
Menus, 44
Message pads, 34, 62, 64
Messages, 7, 26–27, 65
Mirrors, 12, 69
Modeling, 7–8, 17, 19, 33, 35, 43, 57, 61, 63, 65, 68
Mustaches, 43

N

Name badges, 56
Name tags, 15
Negotiating plans, 8, 50–51, 58–59, 62–63, 66–67, 70–71
Newspapers, 19, 44
Nonfiction texts, 9, 28
Notebooks, 8, 15, 30, 40, 50, 60
Notepads, 8, 15
Notices, 8
Number recognition, 24–25

O

Observation skills, 7, 18–19, 48–49, 52–53, 56
Oral language skills, 7–9, 12, 42–45, 48–53, 58–65, 68–69

Organizers, 22, 64, 68
Organizing, 9, 16–17, 22–23, 32–33, 42–43, 48–53, 58–59
Outdoor activities, 13, 24–25, 48–51, 53, 61

P

Pagers, 60
Paint, 18, 42, 48
    watercolor, 46
Paintbrushes, 18, 42, 48
Pans, 28
Paper
    blotting, 46
    carbon, 43
    card stock, 24, 28, 34, 48, 66, 70
    construction, 24
    patterned, 70
Paper bags, 18
Paper plates, 16
Personal development, 8
Phone books, 60, 62
Phonemic awareness, 24, 26–27, 36–37
Phonetic awareness, 9, 30–32, 34–35, 40–41
Pictorial recipes, 29
Picture dictionaries, 45
Pictures, 32
    aerial, 52
    children, 12, 69
    cooking tools, 28
    family members, 12, 69
    food, 16, 28
    license plates, 24
    old documents, 46–47
    people around the world, 44–45
    places, 50
    rescue services, 60
    signs, 48

Planning, 50–51
Plastic bags, 18, 26, 56
Plastic containers, 26
Plastic cups, 36
Plastic spoons, 36
Play, 7
Police helmets, 60
Postcards, 30, 38-39
Poster board, 24
Posters, 8, 12, 33, 56
Print conveys meaning, 9, 16–19, 22–23, 26–27, 30–31, 40–41, 44–45, 56–, 70–71
Printers, 62
Puppets, 61

R
Reminder sheets, 22
Rhymes, 9
Ribbon, 26, 46
Role play, 9, 19, 30–31, 34–35, 38–39, 42–43, 52–61, 64–71

S
Sand/water table, 26
Scissors, 16, 18, 24, 48–49, 66
Scrapbooks, 32, 33, 49
Scrolls, 46–47
Sealing wax, 47
Seed catalogs, 56
Seed packets, 56
Seeds, 56
Self-confidence, 7–8, 12, 14–15, 20–21, 36–37, 60–63, 68–69
Sequencing, 9, 16–17, 22–23, 32–33, 42–43, 48–55, 58–59, 65
Sequins, 70
Shoeboxes, 27, 39, 58
Shopping bags, 18

Signs, 19, 48, 57
    dual-language, 49
Social development, 8, 38–39, 50–51, 58–59, 62–63, 66–67, 70–71
Songs, 9
    "Oats, Peas, Beans, and Barley Grow," 57
Sorting, 17, 35
Spoons, 28
    plastic, 36
Stamps, 38, 54, 66
Staplers, 20, 24, 66
Stethoscopes, 58
Stickers, 24, 54, 56, 70
Sticky notes, 22, 30, 60, 62
Stories, 9, 22–23, 54–55
Story elements, 9, 54–55
Storytelling, 9, 30–31, 54–55
Streamers, 70
String, 24, 26, 34
Stuffed animals, 30, 58, 71
Style books, 68
Swipe cards, 64
Symbols, 7, 48–49, 70–71

T
Tablecloths, 46
Tables, 24, 67, 69
Tactile experiences, 36–37
Taking turns, 8, 30–31, 58–59, 62–63, 70–71
Tape, 16, 26
    duct, 24, 36
    masking, 18, 24
Teddy bears, 58
Telephones, 34, 58, 60, 62, 64, 68
Tents, 43
Thermometers, 58
Tickets, 51, 66

30 Fun Ways to Learn About Writing

Toy packaging, 16
Toy people, 48, 51
Toy vehicles, 24, 48, 61
Transitions, 15, 37
Travel guides, 51
Trucks, 24

V

Velcro boards, 17
Velcro, 16
Vocabulary, 8–9, 17, 42–43, 50–51, 64–65

W

Washable ink, 46
Watercolor paint, 46
Waterproof markers, 18
Wheeled toys, 24–25, 59

Whisks, 28
Whiteboards, 8, 21
Wigs, 43
Wizard hats, 54
Word banks, 16
Word lists, 12
Word walls, 17
World understanding, 9, 44–45

X

X-rays, 58

Y

Yard sticks, 12

Z

Zipper-close bags, 36